I0840997

FREEDOM SPEAKING

POLI-PSYCH MYSTERIES

Karen Kellock Ph.D.

**Manual for
Superior Men**

**This is a complete theory based on Einstein physics,
Political Psychology, Systems Theory
and Archetypal Psychiatry.**

FORMULA

**All success attraction
All disease obstruction
All recovery elimination**

You must fast on all three

OBSTRUCTIONS:

**People
Habit
Food**

CHAPTERS

FREEDOM SPEAKING

Politically correct talk restricts thought and proves we're going into total tyranny as America rots. Perverts are teaching infants how to think--parents weren't watchmen of schools run by finks. They do terrible things for the "greater good": progressive hoods. The human spirit always rises against tyranny so keep that in mind when called "bigotry". The desire for liberty is a tidal wave divinely led as all tyrants drop dead. Contains: POLI-PSYCH MYSTERIES

FREEDOM SPEAKING
Tolerance Means Censorship

Politically correct talk restricts thought and proves we're going into total tyranny as America rots.

Perverts are teaching infants how to think. Parents you weren't watchmen of these horrible schools/finks.

The human spirit has always risen against tyranny! Keep that in mind when hearing words like "bigotry".

Barry brought in immigrants who hated American culture. Can you believe it about that vulture?

COMING INTO A DARK WORLD

We were going into a world so very dark. Where it used to be opulent and free now it was crazy and stark.

They did terrible things always for the "greater good". That's always what they say: progressive hoods.

We can fix the country in a velvet revolution of ideas. It's the power of moral high ground and Jesus.

The spirit of liberty can spread. This tidal wave is divinely led as all tyrants drop dead.

Far left tyranny: If's cool-aid time: groupthink. If you're not IN you're mocked as a bigot and a fink.

Jerry Seinfeld has rejected speaking in the universities due to their Politically Correct tyranny.

Fox News is only 50% truth and that's not enough! Get all you need only by being a headline sleuth.

FREEDOM SPEAKING

Obama's just a front man for a predator group bringing down this country, groomed with lots of money.

Obamanoids would do anything for their god. It's a sign of how far we've fallen by all things called "mod".

They were the saddest eight years of my life but I sure learned about government crimes, rife.

I've always loved high boundaries/privacy but now see these as Godly inalienable rights, you see.

THE MAJORITY DIDN'T MATTER ANYMORE

The majority didn't matter anymore, it was back-room deals not what happened on the floor (political whores).

The New Tolerance has created a nation of perverts, thieves and liars. Reject low doctrines--go higher.

He sold us out overseas, gave nuclear reactors to China and was trained from the beginning, see?

Obama con-gamed us as prey. He hated us and our family--shutting down power plants and jobs, ok?

He sold us out to our enemies, Jesus! It was the biggest form of betrayal and entirely treasonous.

The key to turning things around is vision. We could return to liberty were it not for our history's revision.

The dense in power minimize the dangers of the hour. It's spreading like cancer and soon it'll hit ours.

Liberals imagine "Christian terrorists" everywhere. Don't give into this--they're gentle/deep in prayer.

Criminals love to brag. That's how the tables turn--eventually--but in the meantime it's a drag.

FREEDOM SPEAKING

Forced Diversity is Actually Anti-White Racism

Racist liberals say we're "too white" and many are dumb enough to give into this leftist commie blight.

Trump is the shining light on the hill after all this hell. We've been put through the mill but now we'll do swell.

Bad reactions to Trump demonstrate what we've been through for decades--social hypnotism and tirades.

Common Core makes kids hate everything worth living for. It's dirty, leftist and makes learning a bore.

Isn't it ironic how the Trump-haters have joined Jane Fonda (that commie from the sixties) and Madonna?

CAN'T BE LIBERAL AND CONSERVATIVE TOO

You can't be conservative and a "social liberal" too, since that's murder and perversion, to name a few.

Attacking Trump is attacking common sense. Remember, this generation is public schooled (dense).

Trump can't be bought. He's the answer to D.C., filled with ROT. Gotta love him--how can you not?

Global warming? Give me a break! We all know that's fake cuz green tyrants/elitists are on the take.

The minute they say they're concerned about global climate change I withdraw feeling estranged.

Climate change is just a way to usurp power and have total control. A world tax--that's their goal.

That liberals are liars is proven by how may love Barry and Hillary not caring that they lie.

If candidates aren't speaking against the police state, what good are they?

FREEDOM SPEAKING

We want rights, freedom, liberty.

Spending, entitlements, regulations and debt. Overwhelm the system, capitalism dies and we're dead.

When liberals are in control we have night-raids and kidnappings--it's Chicago-style politicking.

After so much pain and anguish, wasn't Trump a breath of fresh air and answer to prayer? Trust--did we dare?

WE'RE LOSING OUR RIGHTS

We're losing our rights--do you even care? Are you trapped in sin and denial as things fail everywhere?

Christians outspoken on social issues get the blues and shutdown revenues—gotta fight, can't just cruise.

It's not the same country, dummy. it's a criminal takeover by offshore banksters all about money.

We've all been trained to see the right as evil and the left as good--how we have misunderstood!

Women love their doctors because the pushers suggest, justify and encourage these pill poppers.

Please help us Father cuz we're going down. If little ol' me is in Your plans, help me do it God!

Black jobs are being taken by illegals--so minorities love Trump who is exploding in appeal!

America's about the individual. A group's not to blame for one and for ourselves we are responsible.

The more they put him down the more he has grown. That's our Donald fighting idiots all around.

FREEDOM SPEAKING

Say what you want, Trump focuses on the right things: (1) Immigration (2) National Security (3) Jobs.

De Caprio's on the wrong track but with his money he can FORCE his will though it's falsehood, not fact.

You realize how stupid most are in relation to you. You've studied and to principals you are true.

Trump's latest surge is the greatest thing. The more they put him down the more he rises up: the king.

They don't love it--just terrified into accepting it. That's how it works with sadists in control--the pits.

POLITICAL CORRECTNESS TAKES ALL OUR TIME

It takes too much time to be politically correct. We're in too much trouble and are without defense.

Remember the Trump-haters cuz later we can question these collaborators and traitors.

Get rid of her! What a relief to not watch FOX anymore: got my life back from the media whores.

The lawless system does whatever it wants and it's not to protect you--just to taunt.

The mere fact they're all after Trump makes me know he's real, so now you know how to feel.

Boycott Fox: They are boring, opinionated and anti-Trumpish--let alone the drag by leftists.

The Donald always wins no matter what and he always comes out as Truth while they are flubs.

Donald's not only going to lead our country, he teaches us how to be. How to act: the gist is liberty.

FREEDOM SPEAKING

It gives me enormous relief to turn off FOX. Busty voluptuous women, come on--it's boring and sux.

Let me tell you Why Fox sux: In being "fair and balanced" they give leftists the air, an evil influx.

The wimped/feminized men of Germany can't protect their women, children or culture: liberalism is a vulture.

Watch Trump on CNN. As a brilliant genius he uses all outlets--why not? Use them though they're rot.

I'm not like Hillary Clinton: if I ever saw him lookin' at other women I couldn't take the unfaithful vermin.

To renounce liberty is to renounce being a man. Jean Jacques Rousseau

Truth becomes treason when you have an empire. Ron Paul

FOX becoming the anti-Trump network so get offa that thing: this will prevent depression from happening.

Feminism has wimped men who won't protect women cuz the latter said they didn't need it, amen.

IT IS NATURAL FOR LIBERTY TO YIELD

The natural progress of things is for liberty to yield and government to gain ground. Thomas Jefferson

A right is not what someone gives you; it's what no one can take from you. Ramsey Clark

Voting for him once I can forgive. But voting for him twice you're a nut and your brain is a sieve.

Fight not with guns but by killing lies. Free the minds of men so they realize it's tyranny to despise.

Power of the People: Advertising Boycotts work!

FREEDOM SPEAKING

If you study deeply, you're scared. Deny deniers who won't study and "have no fear": they're unprepared.

They say Americans won't put up with this. But they will because they're dumbed down/it's all dismissed.

God gives nations a chance to repent and turn back. Though our world went black, prepare for payback.

All news (even Fox) is watered down. If it's not about the police state buildup it's a lie (unsound).

They're blocking all outs and going for homeschoolers next: You will join the grid, conform and never self-express.

FREEDOM IS A GIFT FROM GOD

Freedom is a gift from God, an inalienable right. But you've given it all away, just to avoid a fight.

And what of our freedoms? You mean we're just gonna go into tyranny, oppression and lose all our money?

It was the dirtiest election we've ever seen and the most important. We were at the brink of joy or torment.

Dirtiest election we've ever seen--so desperate they can't keep it clean but at least they freed the marine.

The crime wave is exploding across the United States: open borders have suddenly changed our fates.

Letting felons go (rapists/murderers who will kill again): You could never imagine that way back when.

Mandate to new electees: (1) Stop Barack and (2) give us our freedoms back. That's it--now attack.

If they're not talking about the police state I don't wanna hear because it's that which I fear...

FREEDOM SPEAKING

Good is superior to evil, so there can be a reversal. Bundy did it in Nevada so let that be our rehearsal.

From messiah to pariah that's Obama hitting bottom in autumn: if dissent is common we'll all blossom.

Gutted border patrol and fence, ordered 60 MIL green cards, triggered invasion last summer: O-Bummer.

FLOOD OF IMMIGRATION IS CLOWARD AND PIVEN

The flood of immigration is all about Cloward and Piven: weigh the whole ship down till it all sinks, amen.

The crowd is leaving the left. They're sick of the arrogance, hostility to good and how we were oppressed.

No matter what we want they vote on what we shall have.

San Francisco bums are most aggressive and lewd due to tolerance and ultra liberalism, dude.

Sweden's feminist-liberal government is why she's dead.

Our only future is in the past.

How can they compare a simulated body slam with the decapitation by Kathy Griffin?

Obama did the greatest thing: uniting the right. What a perfect answer to prayer--an upswing, we're tight.

It'd be easy to hate his guts. We just have to realize he's a (weak, narcissistic) puppet as such.

Liberal fems consider Christian men as sadistic cruel dominators but none makes a better friend, amen?

To think it's only 600 people causing all this trouble as they trap us in a bubble and our worries double.

FREEDOM SPEAKING

Must face it--we're owned. Now pray each day so God will beat the foe and keep you on the throne.

Here Mexico sends it's less by emptying it's jails and the liberal pawns call us "racist" as our own dream fails.

Rapists and murderers (illegals) he lets go free--but complaining about this makes a racist of me?

Cloward and Piven: Everyone on the dole then pull the plug, that's how he gets even. Third world, a given.

For liberty-lovers having a liberal over you is a kind of hell. It's a dark, lawless, unseemly, evil spell.

TYRANNY MEANS HUGE BUREAUCRACIES

Tyrannies have huge bureaucracies, departments and unelected czars. It's a giant leviathan's jaws.

We were a force for good in the world. But not to hear leftists say it--to them we're all evil boys and girls.

It is our constitutional right to be free from worry. Cops have no accountability--that's scary.

The dems have morphed. No longer the party of JFK it's now totally criminal and is becoming worse.

A dark cloud is coming over the land. We're losing all our freedoms and traditions--that is their plan.

As we lose rights we go into slavery. It's scary as a nation comes under judgment despite bravery.

Police tyranny is an esprit de corps affecting the group. They joke about the raids--ram in, give scoop.

We all know someone who's been beaten by cops. Everyone's scared whether in homes or shops.

FREEDOM SPEAKING

Crony capitalism is a kleptocracy by definition: It's all about friends, paybacks and blatant nepotism.

It's like the country's in a trance. They refuse to see (don't wanna be free?) so don't take a stance.

Liberal policies go against God and that's why we hurt, why we go into reverse, why we're treated like dirt.

Bibi won along with the world, conservative patriots, liberty-lovers, Christians and true Americans, amen.

Obama thinks we don't have the moral right to intervene--that's "tolerance" of the mean or obscene.

Nations forgetting God are soon forgotten. America: return to the old paths and forsake the rotten!

OBAMA THE BIGGEST HOAX ON AMERICA

Obama's the biggest hoax ever played on the American people.

The human spirit exploded in the Renaissance but has been degraded and dumbed ever since.

The greatest generation is dying out. Please: Restore these old paths for America throughout.

Obama doesn't see American exceptionalism, and it's sad. It's due to tolerance saying good is bad.

It's no more about our glories but "patho-history": learning all about the vast sins of our ancestry.

You cannot control a moral people: To control them you must demoralize them into accepting evil.

It's not racism that's the success barrier it's the destruction of the family and lack of moral character.

FREEDOM SPEAKING

Blacks had it worse under Obama than any other--so how could it be racism, sucker?

In Europe they're banning "blackbird" cuz it's "racist". We're overcome by word and deed-fascists.

If you don't go along with perversion taught to 5 year olds you "hate gays". God help us it's the latter days.

Feminists say all sex is "rape". This isn't about sex but a takeover plan making men look like apes.

Say one word against MacDonald's and they'll escort you out with cops. They want you dead, or flops.

You must stand up against this crap. "Racist", "sexist", "hater" are all buzz words--hypocritical traps.

93% of CNN Trump-coverage is negative and relentless.

Haha. CNN's imploding and the American genius is mocking them, goading...

Go ahead and be outraged it won't influence how we Americans think. We see your duality, you finks!

We the American People love your tweets. Do more, over-ride the bores!

It was just a joke but that doesn't matter--use the soundbite to silence conservatives/self-flatter.

My friends are going back to Italy. They patrol the streets there and know about Islamo-tyranny.

GREATEST GENERATION DYING OUT

The greatest generation is dying out. They fought for freedom but now all their sacrifices were for naught?

They use the crisis they helped to create to bring in the tyranny. It's not just theory--it means money.

FREEDOM SPEAKING

Germany raiding homes for offensive tweets not the sex crime crisis replete.

What a time we live in: ridiculous policies inflicted on populations and a crime to speak against em.

Big gov is a dangerous master: Decisions made at the top (your data) then local thugs do the job.

Police brutality is not about race! They're mean to everybody--whites are killed just as often, or tazed.

We're like the traitors who didn't go along with Hitler: they'll blow stuff up and say we did it--chiller.

It is our constitutional right to reform this government as we see fit. We're sick of evil, we want true grit.

THE YOKE OF BIG GOVERNMENT

Obama's government had become a joke but hardly funny as we went into total tyranny under it's yoke.

They say he didn't know but that's not so cuz it's trickle-down tyranny from this hateful so-and-so.

The royalty are free from the normal rules of the commoners. They say it isn't so but that's all bonkers.

How is politics really handled? If you saw how it's daily mangled your citizenship would be cancelled.

Don't liberals want freedom? Or are they dumb, willingly giving up the happy kingdom for crumbs?

What happened in the sixties was a cataclysmic transformation.

The promotion of western civilization values--free market and renaissance--the media demonizes too.

There's only one reality--theirs--so they assume it's Trumped up/putting on airs. Left is committed to violence.

FREEDOM SPEAKING

Harvard's confirmed: 5.7 million voted illegally.

Don't be overcome with fear. There's so much happening but God above responds to prayer, dear.

The government machine is above the law. It's always been that way but wasn't supposed to--hah.

We're letting it all go and once that door closes we're in slavery--from one in the know.

The point with police: when they do bad deeds, they don't get in trouble--setting a bad example, double.

It's all gangs in government. Mafia style, lowdown politics and meanwhile we don't get our moment.

It's the dirtiest election we've ever seen. They're mean (even obscene) and we must defeat fiends.

FELT I WAS SURROUNDED BY MAD

I felt the whole world was mad but then saw it was liberals all around. That's all I knew: evil profound.

Cloward and Piven: Make it impossible to make a livin' so you go on the dole and they sucker you in.

They aren't permitted to practice their profession. Like all else they're over-regulated into destruction.

The elites want us immoral because that makes us controllable. Repent and leave cities, if you're able.

Wide open borders and no one cares. As the days roll on people go dense again and the alert are rare.

If they can kidnap you legally how can you be happy? Need rights to relax or we get angry, snippy.

They go to conventions to learn of new weapons and it's a giant market for arrogant thugs and local villains.

The progressives want their way no matter what the constitution says. We're losing our freedoms, by the pres.

Ferguson has brought it all to light: what a few knew but couldn't convince-- how the militarized cops fight.

Militarized cops: not "surplus gear" but rather no-bid defense contracts: sad facts why we can't relax.

OPEN BORDERS AND ENEMY INVASION

The borders were open--we'd already lost our country. It was the end marked by invasion, biblically.

Obama was race-baiting to necessitate the "nation stabilization force" which was dangerous though a farce.

This will bring the NDAA to light too--whew! This could be a beautiful thing if people learn to choose truth.

It's the RAND plan to militarize police as a new market for defense contractors (the red carpet).

This is how the liberal thinks. It's how he wants to believe not true reality-- that's why liberal policies stink.

The trendies just see government as a big teat in the sky: Worshipping authorities, they feel high.

The Feds militarized the cops to bring this backlash--so they can play savior not a treasonous jackass.

Leftist stinkers and deathstylers think nothing of cutting corners and lying-- they are righteous falsifiers.

Homosexual lobby makes us so scared we can't say a thing. Now it's guys in women's bathrooms, peeing.

Been studying the militarization of the police for twenty years. alarmed but

FREEDOM SPEAKING

glad we share our fears.

Gov persecution of dissidents is THE sign of tyranny--the IRS and other depts. take their money.

Demand for liberty is sexy and big gov is messy, bossy and nosy--we just want our own thing, see?

Women are running the government and the military too--a dangerous idea being war-gamed by shrews.

Liberal collectivists demonize those wanting to be free. They say what they're told, without a degree.

GLOBALISTS CREATE CRISES

Problem-reaction-solution. Globalists create crises to bring in world gov. to solve it, like mass execution.

Just because we won today doesn't mean it's going away. The NWO will revive it cuz it's high pay.

We've got to get it together--we're losing our identity. That's who we were but it's going away rapidly.

Cops are killing dogs in their encounters. The public is rising up because this really matters.

It's not the cops but the banksters behind the scene. They stay off-shore, don't pay taxes and are fiends.

You can't be a liberal and a Christian too. It's because of the things liberals believe in (makes me so blue).

Do they follow only the constitution, do they see sin and destruction for what it is, do they wanna get ISIS?

Nowhere to escape the runaway tyrant state. Leave an innocent message and you're red-flagged (bad fate).

FREEDOM SPEAKING

They're getting us acclimated gradually: To scary, unseemly things and along with that, weird insanity.

How easily things merge/converge when we're not looking! Asleep, we let our country go, no joking.

Frog in the water: they're getting us acclimated gradually. We complain, they pull back, then tragedy.

TRUMP'S BAD CUZ HE MADE US RICH?

Please wake-up before it's too late. Tell everyone you know: what they call good and true is our mean fate.

Oh, so the free market is bad?

Trump's bad cuz he overcame the witch and is making us rich?

Dumbed, most people have nothing to say.

They violate the law then make us think it's normal--that's the outcome of Americans getting carnal.

Modern rationalization against God: Acceptance is demanded and no other viewpoint is allowed.

Their rationalization is animated by self-righteousness and outrage. It's psychology, life as a stage.

Rationalization demands the complicity of the whole culture--holdouts cannot be tolerated, sir.

Gayness is not just something we agree to and they go away, it's a reconstruction of existence, ok?

Equality is never going to be enough. What is needed is a social revolution from all patriarchal stuff.

Gayness is just the tip of the spear in the oneist-reinvention of the basic notions of civilization.

FREEDOM SPEAKING

Behind gayness is a massive world view of egalitarianism or oneism where everything's the same.

There is no debate, we are silenced: a deliberate rationalization of something God is against.

The power of rationalization drives the culture war--failure [self-recrimination] is avoided as horror.

Weak chief: Won't fight those battles over evil beliefs and even feels intimidated by the thief.

GOVERNMENT IS *FORCE*

Government is force: it's a fearful servant and a dreadful master. It must be controlled or disaster.

The left is schooled to see the right as bigoted, mean and money-driven. Actually we just want freedom.

It's a pagan worldview of millennials and it's frightening. There is no debate and it's volatile/rejecting.

The bible is not a book but the Word of God.

Big bought off, state-run corporate mega churches.

Everything unnatural is pagan and the list is infinite of sick deviations from God's laws, heavens!

Acceptance is not approval but why would you want it, no?

In oneism there is no good or evil, it's all good except for the Christian people.

Their goal is to deconstruct social justice as Christian witness, what a mess.

The new church says private property must be destroyed--Marxist kill joy.

New feminist ministers deconstruct gender, which there is no more.

"All our new visions are keys to synthesis"--what bull is this?

FREEDOM SPEAKING

"Direct experience of enlightenment within, manifested outward in social justice"--falsehood again.

CHRISTIANITY'S SLIDE

Christianity or paganism: the living God or idols below. Christianity's slide into going with the flow: NO!

Do slogans trump facts and logic? Yes ideology changes personalities and the results are tragic.

Become your best-looking through the animating contest of liberty- fightin' and tyranny-debunkin'.

Despite what they say, with military on the streets things get broken and people killed. I'm baffled.

Elites cut up nations as they want. It's all been planned--don't you understand? We're just grunts.

Ultra-liberal states elect same bums repeatedly. Usually with crime people switch parties, but hey...

Democrats engage in election fraud and wanna declare elections null and void like they're God.

Ignore the trappings of power--they don't indicate character despite the man or woman of the hour.

Freedom is awareness of alternatives and the ability to choose. We're losing all that and it gives us the blues.

The most dangerous menace to civilization is a government of incompetent, corrupt, or vile men.

Megyn Kelly has a checkered record now. Putting down Rudy when he was just telling the truthy.

They ruin local businesses by sending their SWAT team (gangs). This isn't liberty it's just their scams.

FREEDOM SPEAKING

Democrats: At first they were "left to center" but now it's communism: tyranny and lying to you and me.

The most evil tyrants are all called "loving". You must see through such tyranny and all their bluffing.

The double-mindedness of the left: They hate the word "anchor babies" but see abortion as best?

Libs look at the antics of Trump's genius as similar to ISIS craziness.

You're so flagrant in your bias you've lost all credibility as truth rises.

CNN so outraged yet they sponsored the park Trump-assassination play.

FLAGRANT LEFTIST HYPOCRISY

Where was the outrage when Kathy Griffin held up his severed head? Left's hypocrisy is flagrant God said.

Here they declared war and Trump jokes back--and he's the instigator?

It's not journalism, no. It's targeting the leader we all chose.

Even Reagan didn't have the gladiatorial directness of Trump--he's so effective they call him a chump.

Just read headlines and get your life back from FOX cuz mixture/omission make it false.

The new stats show 80% of youth want socialism. Are they mad? It's mass murder, amen.

Your stupid children went insane over the smiling tyrant. They were uneducated, defiant.

Banana republics are horrible--you only get what they give you and they're cold and deplorable.

As a conservative you'll see through everyone you ever knew. They were all taken in but not you.

FREEDOM SPEAKING

Even dems are tired of Obama. What has it been for eight years but trauma from liberal drama?

He was primed by his pornographer-communist father. He was brought up Muslim--an America-hater.

He hangs out with billionaires discussing income inequality. That's the liberal game also with Hillary.

Nations refusing to defend the weak and innocent will be judged by their greatest Defender, amen.

TRAITOROUS HOLLYWOOD SCUM

While we were losing our country you guys were obsessed with Hollywood: liberals with hearts of wood.

80% of America is begging the Chief to do something. Their frustration and fear is quickly growing.

The Leviathan government: huge, complex, redundant and corrupt. But God can defeat them, not luck.

Get fit. We can defeat this total tyranny taking over our country if we just see the importance of being free.

God through a David can defeat this evil giant usurping our whole lives. It's by telling everyone, no jive.

Once they start to take our rights, out goes our lights. Little by little 'til one thousand pinpricks builds a fight.

True liberals would stand up for civil rights of Christians--but now it's progressives, mental midgets.

Our friends don't trust us and our enemies don't fear us as our president has thrown us under the bus.

For every baby slaughtered there's another border crosser and God's wrath can't get any grosser, no sir.

FREEDOM SPEAKING

Everything a tyrant says is always in reverse. Like "freedom is slavery": slogans so terse.

Hasn't he done enough to us--he needs to take our internet too? But then that's what all dictators do.

The whole reason "he" got in was due to the schools being a trash bin and evil liberalism seen in our kin.

In wicked generations the voters are so dumb they actually vote for those who look good, though hoods.

JUDGES BOUGHT OFF ALL LEANING TO THE LEFT

When the judges are bought off and they all lean left, what can we do--as innocents are jailed too?

You simply must ignore what's going on, after learning it. God still has a huge destiny for you, live it.

He's beaten the American public into a pulp. These aren't true leaders--they're just a mean cult.

They groomed him for years, he was perfect as he brought many cheers but now we're sad in our beers.

He loves mean tyrants and dictators. Why? This extreme end of distrust defines all such traitors.

Universities are liberal, financed by the middle east. They all hate Christians and this never ceased.

It's a sad day when we look forward to death. It wasn't supposed to be this way, destroyed by the left.

Now they're putting vaccines in the food! We're to have no escape as our insides are seared and stewed.

We need our guns because they'll invade your home and strap you down--the opposite to renowned.

FREEDOM SPEAKING

Hillary: Take a concrete step to ease the pressure, wait out the storm. For Clintons, that's the norm.

Why would a woman have an advantage over a male candidate--just cuz she's not a man? Silly, a scam.

The true equalizer for women, the elderly and children is guns--which Obama wants to ban, hons.

Social stigma causes shame and guilt. It's a mental mazeway blocking books written or buildings built.

There's so many scandals and crimes we've become jaded. We've given up: all our plans have faded.

In condoning evil men they show poor character. Leave it at that, it's not about their color.

DEGENERATE ARISTOCRATS

Aristocrats: intrigue, degeneracy and corruption are common. No rules, they are the lawmen.

President Netanyahu of Israel we all support you but for some strange reason they refuse to.

Cloward and Piven: get em all on the dole then pull the plug to sink the whole ship.

The liberal fascists seem sweet, humble and helpful. They look good too but oh how they meddle.

Scary stuff occurring across the land! The deeper you dig it's terrifying and more than I can stand.

Tyranny is as old as time and they always have hearts of wood while persecuting the true and good.

Though the outcome seems grim it'll all eventually turn out right if you stay in prayer, fasting and hymns.

FREEDOM SPEAKING

Who's the greatest enemy: is it truly the white, married, heterosexual Christian men--really?

I'm choked up with tears as I see America sink in her swill. It's a planned takedown--plan to kill.

There have been times in history when everyone became a sinner. it was like the filthier the better.

Communism always begins with erasing history: Tearing down landmarks of our wonderful story.

Progressives let felons back into our house. It's also wrong to protect ourselves, they espouse.

TRUMP TAPPED INTO ANGER OF 8 YEARS

Trump tapped into the anger we felt daily for eight years. We're coming out now with cheers!

Illegals get out of a drunk driving for ten bucks. Not US citizens--we go to jail and are out of luck.

If you wanna pollute your children for life, send them to an ivy league school to learn how to be cool.

Once something horrible happens they'll all snap back to conservative liberty principals--fact.

It's only due to liberty that you sick creeps get to do the things you do. In tyranny you will die too.

When you leftists finally get what you want, you'll be the greatest victims of global fascists/the arrogant.

Liberals have become mob bullies. It's not enough to disagree, they must punish adversaries.

Church shooting was anti-Christian, not about race. Liberals hate conservative blacks in any case.

FREEDOM SPEAKING

They care about some insignificant punk but not thousands of Christians killed: bunk!

We could still turn this thing around. It would take mass repentance and a long fast for some.

Totalitarianism comes out of collapse. We may go broke but we must keep liberties intact.

Please God protect me from these awful people. it's like a cesspool and it's so dark, filled with evil.

TRENDIES LOVE TYRANTS

They love the tyrants and will go along with anything trendy. These are agreed-upon sins, plenty.

Sexual assault is another hysteria on campus where the accused male though innocent is damaged.

Unfortunates who have lived under tyranny look at uninformed and complacent Americans as crazy.

Please God, this is tearing me up. America was a decent country but now it stinks: fill my cup!

They're ruthless people without a heart. Most are young, consciences seared with a hot iron in part.

They give criminal illegals sanctuary with no thought of our safety, like we're inferior--yes, not maybe.

Old hippies see no evil, except they hate Christians and those who disagree with crazy people.

You aren't a freak you just expressed an opinion outside of theirs and was cast out--now forget about.

You leftists don't know a thing. You've been so severely dumbed down you can't see the evil king.

FREEDOM SPEAKING

Hillary, Barack and Liz are sick creeps (evil kings and communists) but seared consciences can't see this.

Becoming a Puritan in order is an adaptation to the violence and chaos coming across the border.

To be happy, ignore this pope. The kinda PC things he's saying shows he's a Marxist globalist dope.

Blacks and Latinos are basic conservatives but those who speak out are bashed by libs, no doubt.

The order of the early Puritans was a response to 18th century chaos and thus begun America as boss.

GUNLESS ENGLAND THREE TIMES MORE CRIME

No-gun England has 3 x the violent crime using bats and knives. Only guns protect kids and wives.

We've all been taught conservatives are like Hitler and the left is "good". It's the opposite--understood?

Hillary is a phony but the left can't see that cuz they've never been taught to think or see the finks.

It stinks and if they can't see it, don't talk. If they're that dense I'd block--not a part of your flock.

They scare me half to death they're so evil. Black hearts, doing evil when they get restless kinda people.

There is no end to how low they go. it is unfathomable, you know? Fence up, pray for God's glow.

They're trying to kill us with food, water and air. Also teaching our kids to sin and no one even cares.

I can't read the feed anymore--it makes me sick. Things are degrading too fast without a fix.

FREEDOM SPEAKING

It's so degrading turning on the news. The libs are taking it as far as they can and it gives me blues.

I'm done reading feeds cuz it's a cascade effect as it all turns to weeds and we all fall and none succeeds.

Deported five times and comes back to kill again then they let that "poor victim" go to repeat the sin.

They can't get away with it--God's gonna get em back! But there IS no God? Soon they'll see it as fact.

He is pure evil against everything traditional, lawful and American. He's the antithesis of good, amen.

When leaders have been bought off, what can we do? Just repent so God heals our land too.

TYRANNY OF SPEECH BACKED BY VIOLENCE

Since fascists are violent, be careful when speaking against "gays" (harsh haze, very bad days).

They want us so nervous we watch every word. That's how they weaken us: sayin' we slurred.

They're gonna take away everything and change us all around. There's no end to what they'll cast down.

Obama was a herd hero without morals, just another old hippy with very inferior and evil goals.

Liberals can't see evil so they make lousy decisions about people including criminal illegals.

They want democrats and that's why you can't talk about who's crossing-- some rapists, murderers and brats.

It's not enough imposing this dirty thing on us. Now they want our children-- have you had enough?

FREEDOM SPEAKING

We simply must get off of the newsfeed because it's like we're a pin cushion as our heart bleeds.

Mean Michelle O. forces kids to eat bland, putrid, tasteless food. They hate it, wince then dump it too.

The feds want the moral authority to invade the state while financing race war as we take the bate.

Sodomism sees homosexuality as superiority and all traditional marriage as inferior and the enemies.

The culture is now in the toilet. Even little children can feel it--those who still feel free enough.

SLEAZY HIPPIES FROM THE SIXTIES

Sleazy hippies from the sixties: Now they're old but equally cold as they commit crimes so nifty.

Even though it's massive and everywhere you must grow to discount liberal bias or giant crisis.

Christians are the new Jews. The Nazis were pro-homo, into the occult and they felt superior, too.

So judgmental of me (and for good reason) but not Hillary--a major criminal in our American history?

Most of the media is on the left. They omit the news and skew everything to their liberal views.

There's a proper way of doing things, our protocol: to block the spinning in those with evil strivings.

Donald you've made such a big impression on me. Even if you don't win it was fast therapy for free.

Donald, even if you didn't win it's the evoked archetype that kicks us up a notch past the hype.

FREEDOM SPEAKING

Donald reacts off the cuff--he knows just what to do. It's the art of the deal and he can't be moved.

Beware of feminists when they get into power. They wanna kill what you value and they're sour.

Borders, language, culture and family values. All that is lost unless a capitalist raises revenues.

The conservatives of America see outrageous immigration policies and failure to protect the nation.

These crazy Marxian feminists are relentless and through wrong decisions will make your life fruitless.

The complexities of running a business vs. hit and miss, doing progressive things on their list.

IMMIGRATION WITHOUT ASSIMILATION IS INVASION

Immigration without assimilation is invasion and we're up a creek if it continues: damnation.

In sin (or accepting evil ideas) one's conscience is seared. Atrocities are committed in these eras.

Hopeless, desperate losers who wanna be somebody get radicalized online and it's ISIS-friendly.

Progressives destroy--look at Detroit. Feminists do this to the family or men they want to exploit.

He won't be happy until we're totally wrecked. And the youth still say he's a divine elect--yuk.

He's only just begun. Every day's there's something new to lump but we look forward to Trump.

Please God protect us from collaborators and traitors. We feel it happening with all dictators.

FREEDOM SPEAKING

We desperately need a capitalist to bring it all around. Leftists have so turned glory into a clown.

Had we stayed moral we would have seen what was happening long ago. But sin is denial, you know.

There's always a leader but are they bottom feeders? Will they sell you out or keep you free as peers?

My father said "things will get so bad they'll wake-up and cycle back" but he didn't know Barrack.

Enormous hysteria over a flip remark, a mistake--when it's his anti-immigration stance they can't take.

DONALD SPEAKS TO IMMIGRATION-RAGE

The country's boiling over with immigration-rage and Donald speaks to how we feel caged.

Mental midgets laying an egg over a flip remark and they want to kill him yet Donald be chillin'.

Now they let immigrants in to become our policemen—that's how a country is killed, amen?

We needed a capitalist, someone who knows how to deal. Not these people letting enemies steal.

You'll hear all kinds of stories about Trump and none of it is true. They're so jealous of him, too.

Cultural Marxism is destruction of unique history and substituting a bland cartoon ideology.

If you say "all lives matter" you're attacked for being "racists"--only black matters to the fascists.

Living this way (in constant fear and preparedness for disaster) you're at your most intense, yes sir.

FREEDOM SPEAKING

We gave up all hope after 8 years with a dope putting us on a dangerous and slippery slope.

They wanna make Donald look bad! What pathetic jokes as they put down the King, but we're glad.

LIBERALS LIVE IN MAKE-BELIEVE WORLD

Liberals live in a make believe world. It's all a facade of mutual harmony but it's godless, girls.

The only one. You're a fool to vote for any one else--we'll be restored, we'll finally have fun.

FOX News stacked the commentators against Trump! That settles it--we're done with these skunks.

We've been so mad every day and thought we could do nothing but now through Trump there is hope/no bluffing.

I sense he's sincere, a breath of fresh air after 8 years of despair. People know, it's an air.

They wanna make Donald look bad--like a bloated capitalist idiot. Be ready for attacks from nitwits.

We've got to believe in somebody again. We all saw our doom sealed, no one cared even friends.

Donald says our leaders are incredibly stupid--what a breath of fresh air. Logic returned, I do declare!

Look at the government's bad deals--Trump is the only one with this art. Logic returned with heart.

We need a good capitalist--someone who knows about money. Not a cultural Marxist who is loony.

Trump didn't attack McCain enough cuz he wants to take our guns--needs to be more tough.

FREEDOM SPEAKING

McCain was a war hero but wanted victim disarmament. That was us, the unfortunate.

McCain wanted open borders and to take our guns. He threw us crumbs but Donald is the one.

OUR PURITAN BEGINNINGS: ORDER AND DISCIPLINE

Our Puritan beginnings made us a nation of order and discipline: people getting ahead with vision.

We don't wanna hear about anyone but Donald--ok? So stop with the other detractors--they're passe.

Cain's a war hero, captured and all the rest. But he still wants our guns and to allow in the un-best.

Donald we love your conceit. You can be as arrogant as you please having the strength of a fleet.

After all we've been through with you-know-who we see a light filled with fight showing God is true.

Christian families are very happy. The left wants to ruin that with immorality, making things crappy.

We can still come back and overcome the influence of Barrack: We can go to a castle from a shack.

The white man is under attack. A lot more than any of you know--by race you'll be tracked.

He makes us so happy, relieving frustration after such PC crap. We love Donald, even his spats.

Why aren't feminists against Islam and the way it treats women? Hah--they even love it, man.

Under Sharia women are stoned even if innocent victims. But feminists don't complain--just listen.

FREEDOM SPEAKING

The liberal conformists will go along with anything. They're in perfect unison changing with the wind.

Donald is the only one who can straighten this out. All the others are wimps-- they just have no clout.

So all whites are to blame but when radical muslims do something you don't even mention it, lame.

It's not only government demoting the white man but also the wife--he's worried about his very life.

Pray every day to be protected from your government. It's really come to this, maybe permanent.

LIBERALS CONTROL THROUGH REJECTION

It hurts being ostracized but that's how liberals play: mind what you say or it's a very bad day.

By them appeasing our deadly enemies it's the height of ignorant weakness and they can see it.

Donald is a light in the maize. The huge global corporate fraud that he's hep to--I'm dazed, so amazed.

Donald is the only one speaking to our troubles. The others are astounded as his popularity doubles.

Get away from cities, 250 miles from crowds. That's where the trouble is and they're so loud.

They will make you think like them and stop at nothing to do it. This is tyranny by trendies/the affluent.

There's nothing sexier than a freedom-loving woman but that's home-loving, what they're forbidding.

I don't care what you do in your bedroom--I don't want you teaching the kids to do what dooms.

FREEDOM SPEAKING

Iran doesn't do deals with infidels so they'll do a deal for their own interest but ignore all the details.

Please Donald, do not disappoint. For we're sick of deception and have come to a turning point.

All men would be totally depraved were it not for God. it's like the default setting—being flawed.

POLI-PSYCH MYSTERIES
Revitalization Movements in History

PRO-amnesty/open borders/anti-Trump: These are the fake neo-con RINO republicans they're propping up. Germany/Sweden in Stockholm Syndrome and self-loathing as they love their abusers, begging. Jihadis are coming in with refugees and the left seems pleased. Feminists call the West "anti woman" when it's the birthplace of women's freedom. Islamic world has strongest borders. They don't let em in unlike us (easily taken in) and apparently smarter. How is us having sovereignty (limiting refugees) beheading lady liberty?

POLI-PSYCH MYSTERIES
Revitalization Movements in History

GLOBALISM USED ISLAM FOR EUROPE TAKE-DOWN
COMMUNISM IS CALLED "TOLERANT"
GLOBALIST IS GREEDY, CORRUPT AND ANTI-HUMAN
EUROPE'S PHONY SECULARLISM VS ISLAM
ELITES PICK WINNERS AND LOSERS
CAN'T SHAKE HANDS WITH COBRAS
MUSLIM IMMIGRATION BLOCKS FEMALE GAINS
GIANT SATANIC PEDOPHILES RINGS
TRUMP: INNOVATION AND A BETTER LIFE
HE DELIVERED ON IT ALL
COLLECTIVIST WORLDVIEW STINKS
THEY ALWAYS TAKE OVER, EVERYWHERE
COLLECTIVISM IS LIFE DEVASTATION
LIBERALS LOVE OPEN BORDERS
GLOBALISTS READY TO RULE THE WORLD
THEY PAY THEM TO STAB INNOCENTS
IT'S ALL WORKING TOWARDS SHARIA
HIJAB ADS AND MORALITY
ISLAM & FAMINISTS SAME ENEMY: WHITE CHRISTIANS
"RAPE CULTURES" ENCOURAGE IT
LIBERAL WAR ON WHITES
THE FEMINIST TRAITOR TRUDEAU
TRUDEAU'S FINANCED BY SOROS
INBRED SNOBS
RICH OFFSHORE COMMIES ARE TAX-EXEMPT
"UGLY, DISGUSTING, ROTTEN" SAID THE ITALIANS
FUNDING THE VILE
DEMOCRATS IN BED WITH RUSSIANS
HEALTH UPDATES

POLI-PSYCH MYSTERIES
Revitalization Movements in History

WHAT IS A FRIEND

A true friend is not just someone you party with but who will go to battle with you despite the risks.

Many conclude the people they party with are their friends and what a dangerous social trend.

A lot of people will party with you in good times and fare but true friendship kicks in with warfare.

A friend has your best in mind, makes you better by being in your life and stays when times are tough.

I am your friend, or not. It is not something that can be made or fabricated and is often faked, rot.

Proximity--those you work/live with--does not indicate friendship. Stop telling em everything twit.

Just cuz you go to church with them doesn't make em your friends & family isn't either God said.

90% of the time those closest are backstabbers cuz you assumed too much-- not what you want.

My own familiar friend in whom I trusted has lifted up his heel against me. Psalms 41: 9

Just cuz someone is familiar doesn't make em your friend, they could turn out to be an assassin.

Common trends: You give way too much and throw yourself entirely into untrusted relationships.

Giving too much too soon to people who are untested and unproven: that is the common problem.

YOU LET BACKSTABBERS IN

I was stabbed in the back constantly because I let em in easily and so this problem falls on me.

Trusting without vetting marks the sinner who's boundaries collapsed their whole life perhaps.

You don't throw all on the table, you give in increments and watch the response, noting it all.

If you give and they don't respond or care don't trash the relationship but keep the boundary there.

Never confuse proximity with friendship because those closest could be devising an evil offense.

No one can stab you in the back from a distance, it's those closest so be more circumspect.

Backstabbers are those you allowed to get too close. Think about it: every time it was those.

You trust your back to them, you assume they are worthy so get too close to these enemy friends.

I've never been hurt by people from the outside, it's always the inside. I can blame only "I".

Once you leave the liberal prison you're relocating from you never think of those people again.

You will look for them and they won't be found. It's rather amazing about the human pound.

It used to bring me down when people went south but now I'm so used to it I don't give a thought.

The people problems are so basic they are obstruction number ONE: they are cancerous, crazy.

People I allowed in my home or called me "mom" did the most to destroy my life/bring me down.

Betraying friendship gets you killed in the mob and the major catastrophes in life it caused.

FRENEMIES

If it was anything I. had done I could see it but most times it's the devil in them and you're the target.

Attacks may be subtle. They're not obviously against you but they bring their friends who hate you.

These are flying monkey attacks. Watch these when determining friendship--who has their back.

She trusts the wallpaper man and she trusts the gardener and tells em all about her latest bummer.

She's trauma-bonded--boundaries/morals have collapsed--so she seeks friendship with that.

Would these people be your friends in a horrible scandal where your name was plastered asunder?

Most would delete, unfriend and ban me as a clown but real friends show up when you are DOWN.

Watch carefully who comes around when you're down, it's the most important thing I've found.

Together we enjoyed the prominence/affluence but yet when I hit the ground he never changed.

Sometimes we forget who was with us when we were down. Who's for us, who left us alone.

FALSE FRIENDS' FLYING MONKEYS

These are flying monkey attacks. Caution determining friendship--who REALLY has your back.

Then when I rose back up they all surrounded me: "I was prayin' for ya" yah but you weren't here fella.

FRIENDS are there when you are DOWN and this is how we examine and test whoever's around.

PROOF: You don't really have a friend yet if you haven't tested their response when you are down.

Who calls you when no one else wants to talk to you? Who's there for you when costs accrue?

Proclamation: Real friends are never jealous. And you can tell by their glow as you rise up fast.

The only people who came in were taking everything that was left, picking a carcass while it lasts.

It's hurtful but enlightening how people leave the scene when the party's over and funds deplete.

Presumptuous: They presume friendship in order to make demands on my time, attention and funds.

Jealous of your achievements/can't celebrate your accomplishments, ignore your advancements.

FRIENDS ARE NEVER JEALOUS

Your jealous crony is not a friend but a Judas. She's not just envious she works towards your end sis.

You don't want anyone in proximity who is jealous of you. If they can't celebrate your success, eschew.

"My friend's so jealous of me, what's goin' on?" It's a backstab: they're getting you in position.

Firstly on jealousy: One way of determining friendship is to note their response to your blessings.

Jonathan rejoiced in David's promotion. That's a true friend not all of your frenemy hangers-on.

Those memories are all dispersed--it's like the whole incident never happened, now forget it.

A friend sees you at your worst & never brings it up again, never exposes it and loves you regardless.

Always does you well: A friend loveth at all times and a brother is born for adversity. Prov. 17: 17

Stop hanging on to people who are clearly supposed to be gone--not just hanger's-on but dung.

First you realize it's time for them to go, you make it so, then receive the blessings after, like gold.

Sometimes the only way that person can find himself is for you to let him go tho' it hurts, I know.

No explanation for catastrophe other than the tension reached such a pitch you just went crazy.

This has nothing to do with us. She's just using us cuz we allowed it up to now but we are finished.

WHY ARE THEY COMING OVER ANYWAY?

If you don't cut those ties now it'll get worse with them and the horrible mistakes they make: ouch.

They put you on your meds, you were drinking too, you were immature and unprepared: a FOOL.

When it's obvious they're losers and you hold onto them regardless you'll soon lose yourself: ouch.

Why are they coming to your home anyway? Why aren't they busy/not bothering other people, ok?

First he comes weekly then daily then asks to do his wash: loser creep happens gradually.

You spent your life establishing a home for yourself, he did not--he just hung out, a depraved lush.

When the maid starts to give advice you know she's listening in/spying and that's not her place.

To ditch an ailing husband when he's sick: low trick after he rescued you from the thin and thick.

When the maid inquires about cosmetics you store it's clear she's spying and should be fired.

People presume in on your business. They don't have boundaries like we who've been studying it.

They're PRESUMPTUOUS: They presume on your friendship, stuff, relatives and it's too much.

Sinners die early, tho' some are consoled by a long life cuz after it's over they're going to hell.

DISHONOR IS WORST: GOOD RIDDANCE

You wasted your life, your best years cuz what you held onto for dear life was nothing but tears.

Only God changes a heart but you're wearing yourself out doing what only God can do: give it up.

If you must take a year to heal your heart hon', not hold onto someone who is supposed to be gone.

When you've been honorable to them but they dishonor you, you can't get rid of em soon enough.

When he's in your house, fed and protected by you and he dishonors you--he could also kill you.

When I've helped you and you begin to dishonor me, I release you. I release you, I'm not a fool.

DISHONOR ME, I'M DONE

There are many holding onto people who are dishonoring them. This is wrong--learn to say "I'm done".

When the warped youth dishonor me after I've helped them, I'm done--I can promise you, I'm done.

People have become censorious and timid tho' they'll jump on a bandwagon against the livid.

When a spouse cheats repeatedly saying "I'm sorry" you gotta say: go be sorry somewhere else.

Take you sorriness cuz dishonor is heinous not cuz I'm the highness but honor's the highest.

Jesus said a prophet has honor everywhere but in his own home. Those with access are the problem.

To dishonor is to miniaturize him and bring him down to this: a huge dis compared to public praise.

They take a BIG person, squeeze em to a little one/treat em like a lightweight when they'e great.

It's frightening to be miscast or worse seen as subhuman and only the strongest can sustain it man.

Dishonor defined: They've done everything--giving you the world--and you treat em like they're nothing.

The underhanded maid can make a basketcase out of her lady in nothing flat, just cuz she has access.

How far will this tyranny go? As much as you can take, they can't help it. Thomas Jefferson

Many have spouses who are sick/dying. What to do, quit? No you stick with em to the end twit.

The specifics aren't important, all kinds of things happen when the devil's in control. Just forget it all.

Sex doesn't fix things. They just get far more reactive and complicated and we don't need that darling.

ALL-FORGIVENESS IS MADNESS

I was alot more forgiving when younger. Guys put me thru so much stuff cuz I didn't know any better.

The differentiating factor about dating older is you know what you DON'T WANT/what you want.

What you want today you won't want ten years from now. It's best to allow yourself time to grow.

TRAUMA COLLAPSES BOUNDARIES

I was too traumatized to defend myself/assert boundaries which are seen as anti-social by commies.

Home is a safe environment where we can do our own thing and live our own lives free of spies.

Home is where it's safe to unfold. When there's a war under the same roof we get sick and old.

Shut up women, shut up witch. Talk poetry or don't talk at all--I've learned that from all your damage.

A home is wonderful but one person can ruin it. Guard it with your life and vet whoever enters it.

Modern woman has a mind like a steel trap--so articulate she will cut you down in nothing flat.

I don't lie to myself, I wanna know what's going on. That gives me effectiveness in life. Alex Jones

It got to the point where I had to produce or they'd lock me up, then it all reversed with me on top.

Being ashamed for what they have done marks the saints, even though they know they're forgiven by God.

THE FEMALE COMMUNITY

None of the women understood me/they all cast me in a bad light. How could they not, they're nuts.

It was her constant put-downs propelling me to assiduously disprove her once and for all.

The sly cruelties are happening so fast they go right past unless you're a savvy lass confronting crap.

The sly cruelties were coming from the maid herself. She was so subtle I missed it/just got depressed.

She's the cause of my world success by her constant put-downs: rocket-launchers and catalysts.

Once I saw how out of touch and undisciplined they were, how carnal and appetite-driven, I had won.

The left is guided by utopian vision justifying anythin', the right by here and now, what we're needin'.

System Inversions: Forget those people, soon you'll see everyone scurrying around to do your will.

FORGET THOSE PEOPLE

Forget those people, they know nothing. Just their immediate appetites or who they'll be impressing.

Forget those people, for people come and go but God is always with us, that's one thing I know.

His short-term strategy: rise up like he's gonna hit me but long term I rejected him for good see.

He wasn't a beta male, just a wino. Not even a weak husband but a wolf handing her over to foes.

All are busy/happy around the alpha cuz he's self-aware, feigns equality but maintains leadership.

Realize: He never had the skill set to make you happy. It's only more games and makeup/breakup.

Stop fighting past abusers in your thoughts. Realize: you're safe now behind locked gate/walls.

Please, my precious mind is not your data dump. You talk too much, that's my hunch as such.

Mental illnesses occur just as much as physical. Must accept it as part of your past long ago.

I'm not a big man, I can't defend myself and I don't have body guards. All I can do is stay in my yard.

Stop seeing them as people but past actors in your melodrama at that time then vaporizing.

That's just another era, not something to go crazy over or yearn for. It's steps to the Self/World card.

NEEDING LOW SYSTEMS

That's the most low-minded, ego-driven, tyrannical, low IQ system ever and you need their approval?

I won't bore you with details but a long story short, it was bad. I learned my lesson other than that.

If they have someone shiny & new to play with they won't be messing around hoovering old supply.

The narcissist doesn't miss who you are but only the goods and services you provide now.

We're in a massive process of denormalizing: unraveling every standard for racial/gender justice.

I see no reason to relive past events/keep going back. It was just a lower phase, let it go at that.

Learn to laugh at lower phases when you didn't know what the hell was going on—and let it go hon'

Standards were unraveling/being questioned and you a genius tested this to the hilt and fell down.

We who didn't have morality instilled in us had to find it all out for ourselves in a path called hellish.

The archetype of the savior starts out as a madman, a donkey's ass--just see it as a lower phase.

There's not a single institution that has not lost meritocracy. It's all identity and a shame see.

SAVIOR/MADMAN ARCHETYPE

The inversion from worst sinner to best saint was so great, now just move forward, not relive.

Savior/Madman archetype: why go back and relieve any part of it? Don't relive details of a lunatic.

They were mesmerized by Hitler and even started speaking like him, vindictive and mean.

Wives move their husbands to the left. To me that's the worst possible thing, the women are daft.

They're always seeking narcissistic supply, attention, admiration--pathological cheaters in relations.

People are now afraid to demand monogamy. But to not do this is to say: "casual sex with others is ok".

One is not demanding monogamy out of possessiveness, but there's no other way to play Miss.

You're not getting involved with he who always has others on a line--just so he'll never be alone.

First of all, having casual sex with others is disgusting so why would you ever want the guy darling.

You want a high value man, not a high-profile one. A good man wants monogamy and a home.

Don't get involved with anyone who always has others on the line to prevent them from being alone.

They're putting these influences into your life too--little demons changing your behavior in a stew.

To let this happen/let em in you'd have to be so dense but that doesn't mean you're not influenced.

FORGET IT, JUST A DEMON

They are called autonomisms: uprushes from the unconscious, out of control words/actions.

Jimmy got back at me by letting people in, taking their side or mocking me for being an isolate.

You were mentally ill, had a demon and did absurd, wild and ridiculous things. Now forget it see.

You had a demon and were obnoxious, brazen, presumptuous, heinous, erratic- -now forget it.

That's always how they get you, the weak: getting a flying monkey army against you, they are sneaks.

You wouldn't think of inviting others over to do the job, make the hit, insult the twit: how they do it.

No one would insult the town slut because she'd call in her men, her flying monkey chumps.

Never allow people in if they come with an unvetted entourage. This is unsavory and dangerous.

She came with two men and they insulted me the whole time. They were Jezebel's right hand men.

No more roundtable discussions for alpha females cuz they will use every device for putdowns.

News travels fast in small towns so women are experts at sly tongue, hidden innuendo, getting dirt on.

You said a crazy thing, you made a terrible faux pas. Forget it now, you were mentally ill that's all.

These sly social tactics of mostly women are not just downputting but mental illness producing.

WHEN THE HEDGE IS DOWN...

The wires get crossed in the brain with **TRAUMA** then there's a boundary/moral collapse mama.

With brain wires crossed the immunity gets triggered with excruciating emotional highs and lows.

With these people influences you do uncharacteristic things--things you'd never do before see.

With boundary collapse the world flows in unvetted and you become the worst of the lot/depleted.

When women are mean bitches it's hard to forget it and many men truckle to it making both twits.

When in deep sin or bad association you'd better believe you're keeping company with demons.

Tho' I was terrified when they came to the door I let em in anyway because mom said to be nice to all.

He's fascinated with you one minute then soon he's onto the next--another glittering thing to catch.

There's nothing more important than boundaries and nothing worse than a downed hedge, none.

SEX IS AN EARLY HEX

Since men are highly sexed women must be taught how to draw boundaries and when to reject.

But modern women don't--they go with the flow of early sex adapting to men and not saying "NO!"

They fear saying NO would bring male ridicule--ridiculous, old fashioned, hung up, cold fish.

She loses everything by giving in. The balance of power changes and she's lost all leverage from sin.

You're gonna get what you're getting until you tell them you want something else. No input sux.

Long distance relationships are when a couple chooses a time when they will eventually be together.

I had to teach em how to respect me. They all lack skill sets in relationship so always impose, see?

If her baggage is so burdensome it's impossible to be in a relationship always defending yourself son.

REDESIGN AND RELOCATION

The toxic environment forced me to take a look at who I was/where I was going/how to get moving.

Heartache and pain was the motivation sadly. It made me work on myself and alone learn to be happy.

The greatest advancements in my life were born out of horrific pain--way down then way up again.

Extreme persecution from his family and friends was the lead-up to relocation and joy again.

His flying monkey friends/family loved it when they had a new target to release their bad energies.

Take joy when these changes are forced upon you--when chaos, anxiety and hurt boil a new stew.

I like direct communication so I can know to clear the board. Without it I lose interest, bored.

I'm at home with the religious even if polygamous, no one bothers me or knows my business.

I'm not at home on the coasts surrounded by liberals with policies so weird, brazen and disastrous.

Living with religious I never see em cuz they're all in their homes quietly taking care of business.

Living with liberals it was a constant fight for identity as they colluded against me, it was hell honey.

They're never happy, they have to find an enemy. Nothing is ever really stable in liberal countries.

DON'T GO FOR PLAYERS

You're not looking for a player. You don't have that kind of fortitude and energy, you want a stayer.

There are many women chasing bad boys. I was one of em until I grew up and they ONLY annoyed.

I don't want a boy I want a man. Stability, honor, decency, morality, fidelity and taking responsibility.

You wanna play, go ahead I couldn't care less. I want a cozy home not emotionally homeless.

I wanted him there at first. But as I matured I couldn't stand his manipulations--a boy is a curse.

His eyes scanned the environment seeing what he could get from me--he was not above asking see.

I relocated to get away from you so I'm sure not gonna revive it online and open to the devil.

He loved making me jealous. Why did he do this? Because provoking it is basic to the narcissist.

I went through all this--havoc, bedlam, distress--to learn about narcissists. It helps seeing this.

Why don't we want a stable man who loves only one and puts us in stability--a cozy happy home?

The more a man does everything in his power to keep me in my warm/cozy home the more I love him.

Heaven: I love the beautiful luxury of a stable ordered home when everyone gets along.

No handsome player can compete with a stable man who's responsible and not part of the herd.

That's what a real man does: keep his wife and children in their home, warm and protected, joyous.

TRAUMA BONDS WITH LOSERS

From a pompous ass to a couch potato loser: it's all the same to her, a trauma bonded lover.

I'm preventing you from needing in-the-field training about pivoting--and decades of crying.

My mother always said "I don't trust him!" when first meeting men who eventually did me in.

My friends and family always tried to shoo em away but I said "No, let em in-- it's more than ok".

When your friends and family can see it but you cannot that's a soul tie/attachment trauma knot.

Getting em back: a whole course in itself. It's near impossible after strife eclipsed the Self.

HISTORY: I ignored him as bland when with me/saw him as a gorgeous lion when leaving me.

It's a healthy shock to see nobody cares about all you went thru--it's sad but it wasn't WW II.

HOLOCAUST DENIERS/COMPARERS

When I studied the Holocaust I realized my problems were trivial at most. We are all pansies dearest.

Holocaust comparisons are terrible cuz they minimize the depth of the catastrophe in Europe.

POLI-PSYCH MYSTERIES

Even American slavery, as bad as it was, does not compare with the Holocaust. Please get real.

The Holocaust is millions of emaciated corpses piled up, starved, tortured and worked to death.

Nothing compares with the Holocaust. It was a break in civilization, return to savagery, millions lost

Snowflakes: Stop saying "Holocaust" and truly study the Holocaust to finally see humans/true reality.

Tho' Amy left Johnny for a pompous ass loser she kept his name cuz she knew who was better.

There are Holocaust-deniers/Holocast-comparers and I don't know who's worse, both are scares.

Understand why it all happened: You were a bad girlfriend. Ok, did you make the correction?

If you haven't corrected that problem there's no reason to long for that person. See that son.

This was your chaos, catalyst and necessary pain or you wouldn't have been with that creep again.

Energy is very interesting. Make those changes unveiled in relationship and SEE if you still want him.

She's never gonna attend if you don't fix those things. She'll feel it wherever she is/it's a stink.

Thoughts are things so keep it clean. Remember: he may be thinking of you if you're thinking of him.

"MY HUSBAND IS A LUNATIC"

Should I say "I'm lucky to have you" or "I was so unlucky to have met him, it was so unfortunate too."

"My husband has low motivation." But he's supporting you hon' from his military way back then.

"My husband is a lunatic" but he was in the military for twenty years and it's supporting you twit.

No one's pushing me, I. can see what needs to be done. But I wish you were more motivated hon'.

We are all powder kegs taking little to trigger. The stress is phenomenal living in this era.

What I hate about women is how they move their husbands to the left. Dumbheads, arrogant.

Tho' you began as a madman now you're the savior in field or family, that's the archetype [rare].

I felt so much self-disgust, how could I not? But it's also a Queen's disease and now I'm the top.

Think on this women: Are you inviting a snake in for protection? For this is very common.

Just to keep em on the line, nothing more is meant by it. See these signs then you're free of it.

Due to this terrible trauma there.was a boundary and a moral collapse then they finished me off.

I got so tired of being snubbed I found a man to protect me then I was free/he also loved country.

I need exclusivity for health, sanity and simplicity. That means no one else/no fooling around see.

THE LOVE IS IN YOU NOT HIM

MAJOR insight: The love you feel is all about you. They're just the match lighting the fire.

You own the love, not him. He's the current object of this internal flow but realizing it's you is GROWTH.

It's the wound, the pain, the injustice you were born to correct--that's the motivator for the best.

A roaring sense of the injustice/false dogma plus verbal and writing skills equals these volumes.

You must have PASSION: a sense of injustice you want to correct OR just doing what you love.

Where is my pain [something I have to fix] and where's my pleasure--this determines my passion.

To deal with my own psychological/emotional pain I write like this, it's my passion to explain it all.

It's rather selfish: If I use my pain to help someone else then my pain has a purpose. It's passion sis.

TRAGEDY WROTE THE FUTURE

If being attacked by a gang of boys wrote 130 books on abnormal/dev psychology it turned out good.

It's something that chaffs you--must have discomfort. Mine was society and I wrote about it.

What chaffed me was the mixed signals in systems and society, the social devices/put downs.

The polite cruelties, the mixed messages, the treacherous double-dealings/empty status climbings.

This pissed me off and chaffed my spirit until I started writing with a PASSION to tell all of it.

It's called "normal": You are confident when alone but lose it in relationship or other social s**t.

They put me down so I had to explain in 130 volumes how I was right and ALL the others wrong.

I had to explain and show how they made me mentally ill. That wasn't easy and took a lifetime to fulfill.

WHITE SUPREMACIST MEANS CHRISTIAN

White supremacist means Christian, military, conservative, older or the states in the middle.

Since criminal laws had a "disparate impact" on minorities they downgraded them from felonies.

Outa work, need Trump. Floods of illegal immigrants, need Trump. Commie crap, need Trump.

If Trump withdraws funding from sanctuary cities won't they just get money from the anti-American Saudis?

The penalty for refusing to participate in politics is ending up being governed by your inferiors. Plato

The basis of genius and health is seclusion from outside forces.

Hating Trump is the in-thing to do and if you love him you'll be black and blue.

We're being invaded by sadistic killers and they're blocking it all with non-issues: the democrat politicos.

No matter what he plods ahead keeping his promises to us, sleeping four hours a day--not much.

I suffered open borders. Every time a liberal came in he brought all his friends.

All heroes thru history took the high road and won.

TRANSITION TIMES SHOW HIGH SYNCHRONICITY

Explosion of group awareness. They found that with monkeys though islands apart: it's the collective unconscious.

Transition times show high synchronicity: one miracle or magic coincidence after another, believe me!

PRO-amnesty/open borders/anti-Trump: These are the fake neo-con RINO republicans they're propping up.

Germany/Sweden in Stockholm Syndrome and self-loathing as they love their abusers, begging.

How is us having sovereignty (limiting refugees) beheading lady liberty?

Feminists call the West "anti woman" when it's the birthplace of women's freedom.

If you love women Islam is the religion of Satan.

Trump could block everybody if he wanted to, he's the President and it's the law which four previous used.

ISLAMIC WORLD HAS STRONGEST BORDERS

Islamic world has strongest borders. They don't let em in, not like us (easily taken in) and apparently smarter.

You'd risk the lives of millions of Americans over the slight inconvenience to a few visitors: traitors!

All through history we see Rivitalization Movements changing history under a charismatic leader, our victory.

P. S. Jihadis are coming in with refugees and the left seems pleased.

If banning Muslims makes them kill us, why would we let them in? Why reward em: more killing comes from submission.

Open borders = not a sovereign nation. The left thinks they can have it both ways but they can't: indignation.

POLI-PSYCH MYSTERIES

Real Americans voting for Trump are demeaned, but fear spreads in L.A. as alien arrests become routine.

Would an illegal immigrant protest for you if you got arrested? No, so get real you justice-warrior twisted.

They call Trump's alien-crackdown "unprecedented" because Obama never followed the law (demented).

The crazy left has aligned with Iranians who want to kill us. Liberals are traitors but you don't see em as viscious?

ELITES SELL US BONDAGE, DIVISION AND SERVITUDE

Iran hates us cuz they can't believe anyone could be so stupid as to make a deal like that: Obama/Biden are rats.

Soros and the globalists had this whole thing planned from the beginning: the little pink hats (no kidding).

World government is selling us bondage, division, servitude and lies--why would anyone want this, guys?

Poland was run over by Russia and the Nazis but by muslims hundreds of times, just read history.

Elites are panicking at the joy of people coming together as the dark leaves and the light takes over.

Globalists know you love the NFL so poison it, but like a snake eating it's own tail we'll be rid of it.

Globalism: An elite organization seeking to reduce population in a race to the bottom through consolidation.

When government goes rogue they manage whole populations and skim off the top. That's California, rot.

Dems are going hard left: the socialist takeover of their lifetime, their last hurrah, the last try/their crest.

Playing God: If they can make a sterile society they control everything: food, babies, traits, family.

He gassed, starved his people and bombed hospitals: despicable yet liberals rebel when real men attack hell.

Civilized: People act civil and decent and aren't killing each other like what we see in the recent.

Renewal: A new surge of optimism is putting impossible dreams firmly within our grasp. Donald Trump

Buy gold and silver to store up value in a compact space cuz the dollar will be gone in any case.

Take away our cheap supply of energy and you destroy quality of life and lower life expectancy.

SCHEMES AND SCAMS LIKE GLOBAL WARMING

Schemes and scams like global warming destroyed untold wealth, jobs and opportunities.

We're in dire straights unless we teach prosperity: "You came from Venezuela, no vote communista."

Wherever socialism was adopted it has delivered anguish, devastation and failure. POTUS to UN

Venezuela: This corrupt regime destroyed a prosperous nation by imposing a failed ideology. The Potus

Tho' high enough to avoid rising ocean levels the real trouble is living around millions of hungry people.

Elitism: They're all tax exempt so run their scams knowing they have 3rd world people pouring in without end.

Liberals look at the third world as to what to aspire to, to be. They want to be like Calcutta, see?

Liberals wanna turn us into a Cuba, or Venezuela, or North Korea--but first they gotta kill America.

Build your own economy and move away from the parasites. Cuz they need you when only God can suffice.

New immigrants are used to truckling to authoritarian regimes so they bow down to diBlasio and Coumo.

Progressives see themselves as "world citizens"--not of the United States.

The Muslims need more "support" because one of their members just blew up a bunch of people.

When men are wimps women placate the invaders--it's a Stockholm Syndrome device with rapers.

Globalism is an utterly wicked anti-human monopoly system.

AN EVIL IDEOLOGY CALLED RELIGION

Evil ideology called religion: Extreme Islam is so perverse/satanic it meshes with the left, but don't panic.

Hillary says we can't inflame a religion of a billion people. So appease, appease, lay down to evil.

The bigger problems get in France the more the system punishes those who point out the contrast.

Islam apologism is the greatest threat to western democracy today.

They say "just get used to terror" but that's capitulation, an error.

The globalist liberal subculture is heavily pedophiliac. TV's normalizing it, yuk!

"Unite against hate" is against us, not Islam. It's against conservatives not violence and bedlam.

How the heck is diversity our strength?

Mass immigration with out integration = disunity, violence and depression.

Just be accepting of their cultural ways. "You don't wanna be 'unaccepting' do you?" the liberal fascist says.

If we created safe zones they'd go home for the warmer climate alone.

We have responsibility to protect innocent civilians when mass atrocities happen as in Syria for 6 years.

Globalization uses Islam for Europe takedown.

Hillary sold out country for cash, pay-for-play. Our foes gave her millions but didn't respect the dame.

GLOBALISM USED ISLAM FOR EUROPE TAKE-DOWN

Ottomans used population transfer to keep control of European domains.

They're ok individually but deal with groups and it's a hive-mind situation actually.

Tomahawks are 1 million each = 60 million to make a point, see?

McCain was a globalist for NAFTA, TPP, taking your guns and open borders, EU, Jihadis and wars killing Christians.

"All cultures are alike" is the biggest LIE every perpetrated on a people who stupidly can't see evil. Get real.

Had an awkward meeting with Merkel and that's why we love him, yes sir.

Weather manipulation intends to collapse resistance to the NWO.

Who's pushing white supremacy? It's all in your head missy.

Justin Trudeau a retard obsessed with virtue signaling/Canada is falling.

Tolerance means: don't criticize Islam

Burgeoning of political parties who's only reason is pushing immigration.

POLI-PSYCH MYSTERIES

Why is every Western democracy labelled "racist"? It's a conspiracy sis.

"Hopelessness, social exclusion and injustice" is why they murder/molest?

The least fascist country Holland is called "fascist" by Erdogan the dictator.

Merkel called for "as many migrants as possible", that's all.

The use of population transfers for leverage and to maintain dominions.

"Dual Citizenship" means Turks abusing Dutch welfare programs.

Trump wouldn't touch her, the crazy old bag who murdered her culture.

Of course our guy wouldn't shake her hand, that's integrity.

Our pres stood strong in the face of globalist rhetoric, indifferent to leftist propaganda stooges in the back.

A little lesson to the globalists visiting the people's house in the future: This is our house, not yours.

COMMUNISM IS CALLED "TOLERANT"

Communism is called "tolerant, caring, learning, sustainable and just"--all empty buzzwords that disgusts.

Citizens of a foreign country trespassing: know how to play the game and now squatting with out shame.

23% of schools are illegal immigrants and that comes from YOUR property tax friends.

The feds should only be involved with borders not education, that's the states.

Every first cousin marriage lowers IQ by 10-15 points. Imbeciles invading, violent and not too smart.

Putting political correctness over national security.

Globalists: we've been slaves to their will. Trump the nationalist wants to end this but they hate him still.

Islamaphobia is based on collective amnesia of what we've already seen yet already forgotten--heh?

Liberals don't insist on extreme vetting cuz they think all people are good and that's the tragedy

The meaner they are the more liberals wanna give em, even a car.

Insofar as the globalists aim to end all competition they're the shared enemy of all who want freedom.

Wahhabists merging with hip hop gangster culture? How dark and weird: bad character.

GLOBALIST IS GREEDY, CORRUPT AND ANTI-HUMAN

Globalism is illegal, corrupt, anti-human and greedy (wanting you poor to control you): a technocracy.

3rd World. Your only hope is marrying into the local power structure: all about buttkissing not innovating.

The End? He may have an ace up his sleeve, who knows. It's Paul Ryan, the globalists, turncoats and RINOS.

They created the problem: mass illegal immigration leading to civil war and the globalist final solution.

Muslim immigration rolls back the hardwon gains of women in the west but feminists still think it's the best.

There is no end to Muslim appeasement.

Let's put lowith high IQs, different cultures and religions together, make the Germans pay for it and expect a miracle.

Multiculturalism is a complete failure. Angela Merkel, 2010

We don't need aggression in the name of Allah, no rapes, no lynches, no terror! We must stand up to it all.

Crazy idiotic feminists see the hijab as a symbol of empowerment.

Biodiversity (nat. IQ) irritates both the left seeing man as "shaped" as the right sees him as image of God.

The average IQ of some cultures is imbecilic. That's just a fact from inbreeding and no one can dispute it.

Every time a first cousin is married the IQ goes down 10 points. That's a fact/explains why they get outa joint.

Why seek peace when you're on top? (Koran) It's a temporary tactic to become strong then go back to jihad.

Every time a first cousin is married the IQ goes down 10 points. That's a fact/explains why they're outa joint.

EUROPE'S PHONY SECULARLISM VS ISLAM

No longer the eldest daughter of the French church caught between two fires: a phony secularism and Islam.

When seconds count police are minutes away.

Would China let millions in to establish enclaves and defy gov? Not.

China respects dignity and power not that creepy snake Obama who they led to the back servant doors.

Would China let millions in to establish enclaves/defy gov? Not. And now they're friends with Trump--love it.

Got Gorsuch, friended China, took down Assad and Syrians are in love!
Why we must vet: people are tainted by environment but that libs don't get.

Diplomacy with out threat of force is subservience. Greg Gutfeld

POLI-PSYCH MYSTERIES

A symbolic response to the indecisiveness of the past: We're not Obama (an ass).

We're supposed to house the world's criminal population as long as they come here illegally first. Laura Ingraham

ELITES PICK WINNERS AND LOSERS

We've been taught to hate ourselves--taught to cower--as the 3rd world invades our tower.

We are so empty, pathetic and brokeback they can easily take us over: a cruel fact.

Left loves rapists and murderers--wants to keep em alive. They hate babies though innocent, they die.

The white race will never persist with out polygamy or in 20 years we'll be an irrelevant/hated minority, believe me.

It's not prejudice to talk about facts/statistics. That's science but trendies always bash (get their kicks).

China wants Trump's approval so they're pointing nukes at N. Korea?

Preparing a ground war to push out ISIS. Gonna take them and Assad out simultaneously, that's the crisis.

We paid for a corporate empire so a bunch of generals could act tough. Only problem was: GDP cut in half.

They wanna pick winners/losers in a zero sum game--a monopoly so Trump's standing in their way.

The dems have a long history of being in bed with the Russians--back when (of course) ruled by communism.

Trump believes in prosperity for all and that's why elites hate him, they wanna pick winners/losers: monopoly.

Fox News: Obama channeled billions into anti-American globalist groups.

Crazy Canadian said "I live in a country choosing compassion over fear". Welcome Syrians we'll dry your tears.

Islamaphobia: A word created by fascists and used by cowards to manipulate morons. Andrew Cummins

"Good Muslims" are hypocrites in the Koran.

CAN'T SHAKE HANDS WITH COBRAS

If you're not fighting against evil you're part of it.

You cannot shake hands with a cobra. No matter what you do they are there with an agenda--to erase you.

There's a global depopulation plan and it's not just abortions--also chemtrails and vaccinations.

Just listen to Trump and the wise, not clueless witches and presstitutes bought by globalists/full of lies.

Prepare: guns, gold, ammo, food/water.

We had a wonderful Christian family with scholars/preachers but then a Hindu was grafted in with all new leaders.

Islamaphobia is a device for imposing Shariah. Pamela Geller

A culture is judged by how it treats the least of us: cats and dogs.

Pope Francis is a horrible demonic anti-Christian slug. Alex Jones

Paul Ryan is a bigger enemy than Hillary funded by Soros for treachery.

Paul Ryan and Jorge Ramos are sociopathic con men. Alex Jones

MUSLIM IMMIGRATION BLOCKS FEMALE GAINS

Anti-Trump activist/Shariah supporter leads women's march. Wanting female oppression, she carries the torch?

Swedish news policy: always hide facts about illegal immigrant crimes and only expose those of whites.

"Ethnic rape censorship" is the liberal policy: see it, bite your lip.

Injections of vaccines with trojan horse additives to control populations.

In the view of Jade Helm you're either "hostile" or "permissive".

With photo-recognition software they can find you anywhere.

Under new Agenda 21 standards you'll make $4 a day and considered elite (high pay).

Globalism has killed millions and threatened the sovereignty of the U.S.

Terrorists are always attacking expensive getaways. Stay home, don't be crazy.

We are witnessing the fall of Europe. They've reached a tipping point -- the point of no return.

Because of those promoting unity we've never been more disunited.

GIANT SATANIC PEDOPHILES RINGS

Is the Catholic church a giant satanic pedophile ring at the top?

They don't wanna peg a group. In fear of stereotyping an eagle's no better than a chicken coop.

Phoenix eliminated sanctuary city policy and crime went down 25% instantly.

Got so much power from pedophile cover up he blackmailed to become pope Pedophiles in a satanic network run the country: unreported tragedy.

Pedophilia is just the gateway drug to satanism, human sacrifice and devil worship.

Pope is disgusted by Europe's Christian roots but loves Islam which allows the lewd.

Trump: 10,000 pedophile arrests in America but fake news is nowhere.

Yes we had slavery but so did most other civilizations. What distinguishes us: we warred for abolition.

Learning about France is "eurocentric" but it's ok to learn about primitives: thus we were pulled back.

The biggest lie of the century/history of the world: All men are equal. Born equal some become uncivil.

BBC praising people who wanna shoot Trump.

Youth all over the world finding solace in new nationalism.

The tide of this unelected monstrosity is going out quickly. Soon we're free of the globalist tragedy.

Trump's whole history has been tied to main street not Wall Street. If we won, he won [sweet].

Trump is national prosperity. The globalists want a giant underclass of poor: planned austerity.

TRUMP: INNOVATION AND A BETTER LIFE

Innovation and having a better life is a bad thing?

Man's potential is unlimited/gold vs. a global elite who is consolidating control.

There are times in history where more happened to change mankind's trajectory than in one century.

Elites wanna horde advance tech for themselves but Trump said we'll explore it all together as pals.

The smog in the 50's-70's was turgid. It's been cleaned up so let that go, stupid.

Trump: If we're not doing good, he's not doing good. Globalism: picking winners/losers: falsehood.

POLI-PSYCH MYSTERIES

In Medieval societies the elites decided who could even engage in commerce/loyalty came first.

It's either the free/open Renaissance or the crony capitalist collectivist model making us all dense.

Collectivism manifests as communism, socialism/Islam: cults of power from conquest not innovation.

"Competition is a sin": by John D. Rockefeller, one of the first controllers.

We will no longer surrender America to the false song of globalism. Donald Trump

If a foreign power wanted to weaken America they couldn't do better than Hillary's agenda. POTUS

I think what the Chinese have done is really smart. Hillary Clinton

When we abandoned "America first" we built up other countries, not our own. Trump

Their image of the future was a boot stomping on the human face forever.

HE DELIVERED ON IT ALL

Imminent catastrophe: Globalists sworn to secrecy while we're fooled by the mainstream media.

Since the globalists are used to picking winners/losers, if Americana succeeds it's over for posers.

He delivered on trade, economy, supreme court, 2nd amendment, military, ISIS, veterans, borders.

Globalism is nothing more than a planetary form of colonialism.

World leaders respect Trump cuz he's pulled outa globalism which makes the whole world a dump.

POLI-PSYCH MYSTERIES

Pagan romanticism: the worship of nature. Beginning with Jung this was the Christian departure.

The Christian church became pagan since the sixties through Jung's "romantic synchronicities".

Paganism: man no longer needed God--he'd come of age--but he inevitably failed as a fake sage.

Death of God theologicans [paganism] freed the west of the "tyrannical imperialism of monotheism".

Death of God heretics say God will be replaced with the gods and goddesses of Greece and Rome.

Pagan: All is one. Christian: All is two, Creator and created.

The fundamental anti-Christian [Hindu] notion is "not-two".

COLLECTIVIST WORLDVIEW STINKS

Oneism: All is one, no distinctions, made of same stuff, all just energy, good/evil the same, no tragedy.

Oneism: Since all is one, there is a tolerance for all lifestyles and no difference between genius/imbeciles.

Hey-ho, what's you know, western civilization has got to go: 60's hippie song.

Interfaith mysticism and social justice ideologies are the two forces driving occult spirituality.

The collectivist worldview stinks--it's so ingrained libs get violent just cuza how we talk and think.

A secular humanist liberal denies all the biblical miracles.

Trying to find universal mysteries rather than the Father of you and me.

Emergent Christianity [unity] to be the dominant view by 2050.

Emergence is a paradigm shift rewriting theology and is "bigger than Christianity"--that's what they think.

They see emergence as "more mystical" than what has been--a fake call.

Emergent church sees "experience" as a higher authority than scripture. It's subjective for sure.

It's amazing how they go along with this stuff and still call themselves Christian, as if fluff's enough.

The emergent church mystic promotes "non-dual thinking", the Hindu paradigm which is now shifting.

Emergent church: a great apostasy growing like a weed, my oh my...

A loving God who blesses and punishes is a "damnable fool and ugly God" to these new Gnostics.

What we saw in Poland was sanity returning: with the will, history and capacity to start winning.

They've brought in ten million Muslims to Europe--ten million running around insanely, rapers.

Stone age cultures out of war, slavery, caravans, kidnapping, mass murder and Islam are brought in.

THEY ALWAYS TAKE OVER, EVERYWHERE

It's not about working or having a job, it's about politically taking over and that's what the Muslims do, God!

I pray the new Trump/Putin alliance will change the balance of power to eliminate the Jihadis forever.

It's like the arrogant Macron, declaring himself a Jupiterian God to rule with an iron rod and Martial Law.

Evil wants to destroy Russia and the U.S. cuz Christianity is coming back in these nations, yes?

Jesus said the gates of hell would open but they wouldn't prevail. Think of that when you fear to fail.

Mass denial from political correctitude has lifted and across the world in all countries attitudes have shifted.

It is their religion, darnit! It is their holy book that says to go do those things—get hep!

Importing ready-made voters rather than making the case to the American people about free loaders.

Trumpsters fuming over his apparent reversal on dreamers.

For every dreamer there's an American who needs a job or education.

It was anti-immigration/political correctness that we voted for. If he goes soft on these things = war!

Communist China owns Hollywood so of course they demonize/lie about us constantly, that's understood.

Trumpism: Americanism not Globalism.

London is left of center, labor. So it's murdering mayor compares our leader to ISIS horror!

COLLECTIVISM IS LIFE DEVASTATION

Collectivism--whether fascism, nazism or communism--is life devastation so fence me in from em.

Tho' London caved the rest of Britain is Trumptown: they want sovereignty from EU and won't back down.

London (Obama on steroids) is lost to liberals and it stinks not confronting terror and not giving links.

J.K. Rowlings writes fantasy books so she says "England is united"--what a crock and how crooked.

POLI-PSYCH MYSTERIES

We've been paying the pirate so long it's now a huge baby crapping all over us. Alex Jones

Build a wall and encourage the tens of millions here to self-deport.

Defeat amnesty or lose the republic cuz they will always vote big government and we'll lose it.

LIBERALS LOVE OPEN BORDERS

There are those who think it's noble to have open borders. Left likes cheap votes, right likes cheap labor.

Putin has an 85% approval rating/his people love him and he's a Christian-- that's why liberals hate him.

Russia and America have the same enemies and forces trying to bring them down: Soros for one.

It was Putin's help that ended ISIS who were burning/drowning people in a most major global crisis.

They hate Putin for the same reason they hate Trump: He's a real man not a wimp and liberal chump.

They hate Putin as the devil in them hates all Christians, so can't forgive him for past transgressions.

Pentagon called Kim Jong Un a madman and that means you're about to get killed buddy, count on it.

We're on the edge of total disaster or jubilee. What will it be--what leader Trump wants it will be.

Tide is going out on globalism cuz it was authoritarian, crony capitalist, centralized and we hated it.

GLOBALISTS READY TO RULE THE WORLD

Globalists were ready to rule the world but they killed the golden goose, got greedy and criminal too.

Wow: Germany has gained massively thru the EU what it couldn't in WWII: money and control too. Top of Form

Hundreds of countries bordered, unique and charming. Isn't that better than skid row/chaos/starving?

Elitists fly around pretending to be philanthropists giving away people's money: great life I'd say.

They're just practicing their faith but if we succumb to their demands for Shariah we're a dead country.

Liberals now virtue signaling about how the hurricanes are caused by us disbelieving global warming.

It's an all-out communist revolution, the barbarians are at the gates and Obama's behind the hate.

ISIS Claims Responsibility For Mass Shooting: Suspect Converted Months Before

Las Vegas killer had converted to Islam in the last two months--unreported by fake news of course.

I had to transcend the details of tragedy.

To prohibit invaded Europe from defending herself or even talking about it--I just can't believe it.

THEY PAY THEM TO STAB INNOCENTS

They pay them to go out and stab people. A poor family gets a cool 200 grand to commit this evil.

Teleprompter-reading fake news comedians are the new voice of the globalists feeling powerless.

Their enemy are those wanting individual liberty, while they're collectivists who just want tyranny.

POLI-PSYCH MYSTERIES

Globalists have overcome many other countries always by starting civil wars with mass shootings.

It wasn't a white man with a gun it was a liberal progressive Antifa recent Islamic convert with a gun.

Socialism is totally selfish, saying "I'm breathing so you owe me crap" or "I'm better than you", like that.

Always standing on graves in order to push their political agenda.
We all know Vegas was an attack of ISIS

Era of psychosis: We all know who's attacking but we can't say this.

Trump fought ISIS and they fought back by killing 59 people in Vegas.

He was not a Christian but a leftist atheist who converted to Islam.

IT'S ALL WORKING TOWARDS SHARIA

Liberal feminists hating the west/wearing hijabs: Anyone who hates freedom, they love it.

France: Islam seen as religion of the poor--you can't tell em they're wrong or you're an elitist/fascist bore.

People don't object cuz they're scared to death. That's the plan--terrorize us to accept the hijab.

Our own govs ban speech against this invasion. The whole world save a few countries have fallen.

It's all working towards free speech laws of Sharia. Allow that to happen = you're gone, like Canada.

Absurd lies accepted: War is peace, freedom is slavery, ignorance is strength and other stench.

The man has no responsibility for self-control--it is entirely the woman's: what an evil black hole.

Make sure he's not tempted and if he is tempted it's her fault: honor killings.

HIJAB ADS AND MORALITY

Anyone advertising hijab is saying they're all for Islamic morality.

Why ban speech: Islamo-Communist takeover, that's all you should teach.

They know them by their GEAR: The culprits being fans of ISIS all have accouterments of fear.

The target was the motive: Country western, Christian.

GET IT: Banning speech is an Islamo-Communist revolution and takeover 100 years since Russia.

Due to the violence/hatred in the Koran, even if he's not violent he's not against others who are.

Islam is authoritative, violent and supremacist at it's core.

Ours is equal protection under the law but under Shariah, Muslims have preferential treatment.

I'd hate to see us come under domination by a foreign power but that'll happen if we let em in forever.

New feminist movement is Steinem standing with Sarsour: women going into tyranny/made poor.

Islamo-feminism is an oxymoron but it's shot to the top in universities and all wanna belong.

Islamo-feminists wanna cut female genitals off--that's just what feminists love (playing God).

ISLAM & FAMINISTS SAME ENEMY: WHITE CHRISTIANS

Islam and feminists have the same enemy: white western Christian culture.

Vegas was retaliation for Trump's attacks on ISIS.

Canadian driver slammed car into many people but they don't know why tho' he flew ISIS flag in sky.

It has nothing to do with you being Canadian, it's your jerky leader Trudeau who's letting em all in.

Public would be more enraged by terror attacks if they saw the aftermath but the media blocks that.

6000 a day flowing into Italy is a vastly understated catastrophe.

Migrant deluge isn't going to become European--Europe will just become like the third world again.

Merkel says: I'm doing a long plan so put up with the muggings, rapes and slaughter in the meantime.

It's not about Syrian refugees: Floods from everywhere and it's not about wars it's cuz it's all free.

It's ok for them to be with their own kind, but not for us--we gotta put up with the unkind/unrefined.

Liberalism: gateway drug to extreme left

Europeans think if they're guilty of everything and the world nothing then they'll forgive them.

Black Lives Matter doesn't care about black lives but attention, money and like all activists, more money.

"RAPE CULTURES" ENCOURAGE IT

A "rape culture" is one which encourages rape--that doesn't exist on campuses so shut up, fakes.

They're shocked and call false any truth they don't like. Inconvenient truths-- how stupid, yikes.

The era of stultifying political correctness: walking on eggs, making mistakes, giving in, paranoia.

POLI-PSYCH MYSTERIES

The left in America are preoccupied with defending pedophilia (born with it) just like President Obama.

Feminists ignore Muslim gang rapes but they blow up over a campus rape crisis that doesn't exist.

Progressives are morally bankrupt and that's why they must virtue signal constantly, think about that.

Leftist identity politics is underpinned by moral relativism--like gang rapes are ignored by feminists.

Under moral relativism, no matter the barbaric act, we all did it.

"All religions are equally violent". Obama

One disaster after another--clusters--is called "singularity"--from gravitic effects of Nemesis, a rarity.

There is no justification for mass low wage immigration, none.

Gays are getting sick of liberals saying "Islam is a good thing" when it throws em off roofs, ya think?

Slavery is going on right now under Islam but they're only concerned about Columbus 500 years ago.

LIBERAL WAR ON WHITES

To further the war on whites, liberals bring in Islamic terrorists to attack specifically white Christians.

There's now more unity than ever despite Obama, Pelosi and globalists trying to divide us for war.

Once globalism's exposed it can't exist cuz it's unelected, tax exempt and with diplomatic immunity.

Populist Trump revolution is part of a worldwide move against satanic pedophile elites (coming unglued).

"Soros is an agent of Satan"--it's Hungary's Christian duty to get him for turning Europe over to Islam.

Once exposed, a globalist above-the-law tax-free corporation backing authoritarianism is dead!

Globalism is a plague and failure--despite the frothing, agonizing death throes of late night haters.

Despite Ponzi schemes of media/globalists thinking they'd rule the world as Gods, we won/they lost.

Globalism move over: the fall of Hollywood, NFL , both party dinosaurs, EU and the Islamic takeover.

Just a little bit further and the age of the globalists will be over. Our new liberty will be glory forever!

What is the difference between conservative and communist? One means freedom, the other dominance.

They all know they're frauds, jokes, losers and fakes so wanna destroy all that's good for the devil's sake.

Put America first--not immigrants. Why does Eminem hate this—an idiot?

The world's leaders don't care about the people already living there at all! Some do but that's small.

Trudeau can't fight wife-beating cuz that's Islamophobic, in another contradiction of that nut.

Is there ANY line that western liberals won't let Islam cross? No, and they've quickly become boss.

THE FEMINIST TRAITOR TRUDEAU

When "feminist" Trudeau comes to mind what do we think? A battered wife and a bloodied hockey stick.

They won't report rape cuz it might damage welcoming to refugees, ruled by evil and liberal sleaze.

Unvetted: no cultural questions (equality of sexes) or value questions (do you believe in non-violence)?

Of course wife-beating is tied to the refugee policy when we're importing from misogynistic countries.

Poor guy "didn't know" wife beating was wrong because it's NOT wrong where he comes from, duh!

Wife-beating is endemic to Muslim culture so it's no mystery why there are so many female murders.

Wife-beating is hardwired into the religion. It's a specific Shariah punishment--a prescription.

Many naive youth are attracted to the edginess of Islam. You get to rape, beat and marry other women.

They always say "domestic violence is everywhere" but only in Islam is it legal and that's why we care

Duh: Wife-beating is linked to Islam/Muslim-majority countries. What a revelation, but they can't see.

There's always an exception to liberal values (e.g. feminism) when Trudeau enters it's about Islam.

To criticize Islamic law (allowing wife-beating) is blasphemy, so in any fight feminism loses in this tragedy.

TRUDEAU'S FINANCED BY SOROS

Why are all Trudeau's MP's authoritarian Shariah varieties instead of the freedom loving liberties?

George Soros donates 10 million dollars to fight "incendiary rhetoric" but it's all-ok with liberal comics.

POLI-PSYCH MYSTERIES

Trudeau's financed by Soros, meaning the power of the government will stamp out political commentary.

We still have first amendment while Canada has hate speech laws—that's from Soros playing God.

Where science is an obstacle to their agenda they simply abandon it. Libs cut corners/lie about it.

Pamela Geller is named the top world expert in radical Islam, Shariah law and Islamic supremacism.

It's the UN running our immigration program!

Do they go to war because of a burning cause, really? Or to join the foray, for money, to play boss.

How dare us respect our ancestors, traditions, history and culture not suckup to globalist monsters.

Both parties hate Trump. That alone should teach us something about the arrogant globalist gangsters.

Why would you want unelected foreign boards to rule over you? Are you fools? (It's from the schools).

They want to bring in a worldwide autocratic authoritarian system they call a "technocracy".

I know this stuff sounds crazy but they're the crazy ones.

Megalomania in history: old elites inbred and crazy started wars, killed people, played God.

INBRED SNOBS

Being snobs they inbreed cuz siblings/cousins are all they see.

Who is younger Bush kidding? He's just a wretched globalist wanting us on our knees, begging.

Bush says we've withdrawn from "global engagements" which means he wants us caught again.

Bush, Obama, Clinton: Biggest globalists in town--baiting, panting/waiting for their plan to go down.

Bush: European Union vs. "economic stagnation, youth unemployment, anger over immigration."

Bush the moron: a "resurgence of ethno-nationalism hurting the great European Union".

"Bigotry seems emboldened"--shut up Bush you moron for ultimately you just want our guns.

We see it everywhere: people don't wanna be over a big private corporate new world order!

The elites got so busy creating their new civilization they couldn't see how much we hated em.

Globalism's failing as an authoritarian secret system. If we just stand up it falls cuz we want freedom.

We want freedom while they're promoting Venezuela and North Korea communism? Only the dumb

We're winning fast, nationalism has taken over cuz our anti-establishment president is so clever.

Winning: Cuz people are tired of the neo-con globalist duopoly that has ruined this country.

RICH OFFSHORE COMMIES ARE TAX-EXEMPT

Why do the rich want communism? Cuz they're offshore and tax exempt while we stay down/made inept.

Connection of demographics and terrorism: more Muslims, more catastrophe of this kind.

POLI-PSYCH MYSTERIES

After bludgeoning us for eight years with Builderberg orders now creepy Obama virtue-signals.

"Parts of Europe have developed an identity crisis" means we want our own destiny: just us..

"This new nationalism hurts democracy and the individual"--more Bush bull.

Crawl back into your hellish holes, America knows who you really are: Clinton, Bush and Barry O.

These guys are so outa touch they don't even realize we think they're all wicked globalist nuts!

Bush equates the industrial/agricultural revolution with globalism--the most evil tyranny around.

The elites are pedophile perverts and it's all reflected in Hollywood--it's the same, understood?

Trumplike leaders proliferating around the world! Things are looking up so take a vaca from sorrow.

Liberals believe that national sovereignty is not important. They want us all one, in the gutter.

Dictators always promise a utopia for the average person but when realized it's the opposite.

The globalists are devil-worshippers using immorality to conquer us.

The dictatorship of globalists means loss of national identity.

"UGLY, DISGUSTING, ROTTEN" SAID THE ITALIANS

100% of the Italians interviewed called Muslims "ugly, disgusting, bad, rotten--we want them gone".

Disgusting isn't the word for it--they kill dogs, stone women/gays and Europeans are sick of it.

They kill dogs but Trump loves dogs and we want them gone, out, back where they belong!

MUSLIMS KILL DOGS because dogs are "dirty" but they're not, wiping butt with their hands?

Don't you dare call dogs dirty if you do those horrible wretched things smarty.

They wipe with their hand then call dogs "dirty" cuz they're as bad as liberals making no sense.

Thank you Alex Jones for being such a brilliant genius and explaining it all to us about globalists.

Alex Jones says the new world order, media and globalism is collapsing. Have hope, be happy.

This is the ultimate and Trump predicted it: Take down George Washington: it's communistic.

FUNDING THE VILE

Funding the vile: UN funds jihad, Jew hatred, creed/gender apartheid and sharia worldwide.

Look at what liberal thinking has done to Europe: flooded with the dregs from opposite cultures.

Is De Blasio trying to get New Yorkers killed?

The elites think they can get away with anything--like the lowest base acts, but we are *winning*.

Stockholm Syndrome: Woman was raped/murdered by immigrants, mom took up an offering for em.

It's ridiculous to say we're a rape culture when men go to prison but in third world, no incarceration.

The UN likes pedophiles--they wanna legalize it at age 13.

They call me a Russian agent, a kingpin with no evidence. Trump

DEMOCRATS IN BED WITH RUSSIANS

Don't gain the world to lose your soul, WISDOM is better than silver and gold. Bob Marley

Soros calls overthrowing elected governments "pro-democracy" so FYI that's what it means.

A dying authoritarian group--arrogant/used to power--is being removed caught doing as accused.

A quarter of illegals have mental disorders. Our vetting sux we gotta take a break/close the borders.

We must not allow ISIS to return, or enter, our country after defeating them in the Middle East and elsewhere. Enough! Donald Trump

The democrats are in bed with the Russians, the communist Chinese and everyone else.

Why do I have to pat on the back every Muslim who doesn't want to kill me? Pamela Geller

They hate dogs. We don't want dog killers or cruel *halal* slaughter here.

Where are the liberals about that? Not a word.

HEALTH UPDATES

As we approach The End time becomes incredibly valuable/we don't waste one minute ya' know.

While I lay dying I cried out for Jesus--fact--and He brought me back with this Creative Act.

Don't you understand, it's due to Jesus we can be free of it--that includes memory of it: all ERASED.

They turn the power off to show us who's boss. It's how they rule/get wood/don't forget about this.

Cancel culture [character assassination] is a dress rehearsal for mass murder [disappearing]. Stefan Molyneux

100 KAREN KELLOCK BOOKS

AFFINITY OR MISERY
AGELESS CORNUCOPIA
AMERICA AWAKE!
AMERICA'S DAFT ERA
ARTS OF PALEO FASTING
AUTOPHAGY ON CHEATERS
BACKSTABBING NEUROTICS
BETRAYAL TRAUMA
BOOMERS AND BROKENNESS
BOOT ON NECK
CHAMPION GUIDES
COMMIE NUTHOUSE
COMMIES
COMMUNIST SPIRIT
CONTAGION OF MADNESS
CONTAGIOUS MADNESS
CULTURE CLASH BASHED
DAFT LEFT
DAILY FASTARIAN
DAM RATS
DIVERSITY IS CRUELTY
E-RACE WHITE
EVIL FREAKS (Beyond Gross)
THE END OR A BEND?
FEMALE BULLIES AND FEMI-NAZIS
FEMALE CARNALITY
FEMALE DUMB DOWN
FEMALE POWER DRIVE
FEMINISM AND RUIN 1 & 2
FIX FOR MISFITS
FOOLS & TRAMPS
FREEDOM SPEAKING
FRENEMY ENABLER
FRENEMY LIAR
FRENEMY THIEF
FRENEMY TRAITOR
TRENEMY TYRANT
GENIUS IS HELD DOWN
GLOBALISLAM
GOD USES THE FLAWED
HAZE OF THE LATTER DAYS

THE HERD IN WORDS
HIX POLITIX
HOW THEY RUINED US
JUST SKIP DINNER
LE FEMME AND THE COMMUNIST SPIRIT
LIBERAL CHAOS & ROT
LIBERAL DOUBLETHINK
LIBERAL GALL 1 & 2
LIBERAL SHOVE-DOWNS
LOCK YOUR GATE
LOSERS and Femme Fatales
MANUAL FOR SUPERIOR MEN
MODERN ART FROM HELL
MOSTLY FAKE
NOTES TO CHAMPS 1 & 2
OVERCOME FRENEMIES
PC MAKES US CRAZY
PEOPLE ARE CRUEL
PEOPLE PROBLEMS 1 & 2
PERSECUTED GENIUIS
POLI-PSYCH MYSTERIES
PRETENTIOUS SLOBS
QUEEN BEE
RED NEW DEAL
RETURNING TO FIRST NATURE
SEASON OF TREASON
SEPARATE MEANS HOLY
SOCIAL HYPNOTISM
SOLITUDE SOLUTION
SUPERCILIOUS
THE SCHOOLS SCREWED EM UP
TOAD TO PRINCE
TRIALS CYCLES
TRUMP VS. GROUP
TRUST IN TRASH
THE TRUTH ABOUT PEOPLE
UNDERHEANDEDLY CLEVER
WALK TALL WITHIN WALLS
WE'RE NOT ALL ONE
WINNERS SKIP DINNER
WORK OR SMERK

AUTHOR BIO

Karen Kellock Ph.D.

Ph.D Political Psychology, UCI 1976
Post-Doctoral: UCI Medical School
Department of Psychiatry
Grants NIMH, NIAAA

Ph.D. dissertation "A Systems-Theoretic View of Pathologic Interaction" made an early mark as the "Wife of the Alcoholic Syndrome". Postdoctoral research at UCI Medical, Dept. of Psychiatry on the systems surrounding pathology on NIMH and NIAAA federal grants: *The Contagion of Madness: The Psychology of Neurotic Interaction and Pathological Systems*. Therapy tool Therapeutic Playwriting introduced the play *Mary and Murv: Gruesome Twosomes in the Alcoholic Marriage*. She taught Abnormal Psychology and Pathological Systems Theory at UC and CSU campuses and developed "the Debris Theory of Disease" in five books and website: (www.karenkellock.org): *Champion Guides, Daily Fastarian, Just Skip Dinner, Arts of Paleo Fasting, Ageless Cornucopia. Manual for Superior Men is a* pick-it-up-anywhere book that you can't put down (20,000 Kellockialisms) and ever on your desktop it should be found (or this Ebook for superior wordsearch of new jargon).

www.ingramcontent.com/pod-product-compliance
Lightning Source LLC
Chambersburg PA
CBHW061719250726
48657CB00002B/677